PUBLIC LIBRARY DISTRICT OF C

W9-CMT-082

drug facts
INHALANTS

FRANCHA ROFFÈ MENHARD with Laura Purdie Salas

Marshall Cavendish
Benchmark
New York

Marshall Cavendish Benchmark
99 White Plains Road
Tarrytown, NY 10591
www.marshallcavendish.us

Text copyright © 2010 by Marshall Cavendish Corporation

All rights reserved. No part of this book may be reproduced or utilized in any form or by any means electronic or mechanical, including photocopying, recording, or by any information storage and retrieval system, without permission from the copyright holders.

All websites were available and accurate when this book was sent to press.

Library of Congress Cataloging-in-Publication Data

Menhard, Francha Roffè.
    Inhalants / by Francha Roffè Menhard with Laura Purdie Salas.
        p. cm. — (Benchmark rockets : drug facts)
    Includes index.
    Summary: "Discusses the history, effects, and dangers of inhalants as well as addiction treatment options"—Provided by publisher.
    ISBN 978-0-7614-4350-6
1. Inhalant abuse—Juvenile literature. I. Salas, Laura Purdie. II. Title.

HV5822.S65M46 2010
613.8—dc22
2008052739

Publisher: Michelle Bisson
Editorial Development and Book Design: Trillium Publishing, Inc.

Photo research by Trillium Publishing, Inc.

Cover photo: iStockphoto.com/aolr

The photographs and illustrations in this book are used by permission and through the courtesy of: *Shutterstock.com*: Picsfive, 1; hkann, 8; Sebastian Kaulitzki, 9; Adam Tinney, 27. *Sunny Gagliano*: 4, 19. *Jupiterimages Corporation*: 10, 18. *AP Photo*: Scott Sady, 17. *iStockphoto.com*: Quavondo Nguyen, 23. *Corbis*: 25.

Printed in Malaysia
1 3 5 6 4 2

CONTENTS

1   What Are Inhalants? 4

2   Who Uses Inhalants,
    and Why? 10

3   What's Being Done to Stop
    Inhalant Use? 18

4   How to Help 23

    Glossary 28

    Find Out More 30

    Index 31

1 What Are Inhalants?

YOU DON'T HAVE TO LOOK FAR TO FIND AN INHALANT. Inhalants are in classrooms and libraries, garages and workshops, bathrooms and kitchens. If you hear someone talk about *huffing*, *bagging*, *sniffing* or using *glue*, *kick*, *rush*, *whippets*, or *buzz bombs*, they are talking about using inhalants.

Inhalants are everyday products that give off fumes. These products are safe when used as directed. Directions for use warn you not to breathe in the fumes. Yet sometimes people breathe in, or inhale, the fumes to get high. When people abuse these products this way, the results can be deadly.

There are more than a thousand different kinds of inhalants. Some are liquids, and some are sprays.

Do you know which of these common inhalants are aerosols and which are volatile solvents? Take a look at the chart.

4

The Four Categories of Inhalants

Category	Examples
gases: Substances that have no fixed shape and can expand.	propane nitrous oxide ("laughing gas") chloroform ether
aerosols: Gases that are used in spray cans.	whipped cream in cans computer duster sprays ("canned air") hair sprays deodorant sprays spray paints
nitrites: Products that are made from a poisonous form of nitrogen.	air fresheners "snappers" "poppers"
volatile solvents: Liquids that give off fumes at room temperature.	paint thinners and removers correction fluid fluid in felt-tip markers glues nail polish removers

A Different Drug: A Different Danger

Inhalants are legal, cheap, and easy to get. This makes them different from other drugs. This is also part of what makes them so dangerous. Because inhalants are more available than other drugs are, they are easier to try, and people often overlook the dangers. Many people don't think of these everyday products as being particularly harmful.

But inhalants are very harmful. One major danger comes from the fact that inhalants are made from many different chemicals. When people use a drug like marijuana, cocaine, or heroin, they know what they are introducing into their bodies. They have some idea of what will happen. But when people use an inhalant, it is almost impossible for them to know what they are breathing in and what will happen, due to the different chemicals in every inhalant and their different effects.

For example, **toluene** is one of the most common chemicals in volatile solvents. It is also one of the most **toxic**. It absorbs quickly into the lungs, brain, heart, liver, and reproductive organs and causes damage in these places. It also causes brief giddiness, clumsiness, and headache. **Methylene chloride** is another chemical in volatile solvents. It allows less oxygen into the blood and makes the heart beat irregularly. It causes dizziness, sleepiness, and confusion and can lead to death. An inhalant can contain one or both of these chemicals and others as well.

Some of the chemicals in inhalants have been well-researched, but many have not. Therefore, no one knows what all of the effects of inhalant use are. This makes it difficult to treat people who are addicted to inhalants or who may have **overdosed** on them. It also makes it risky to use inhalants even casually. However, many of the short- and long-term effects of inhalant use are known. Here are the facts.

All inhalants act on the **central nervous system**. It takes only about five minutes for them to act. That means people get high fast, and the damage to their bodies starts quickly. People describe the high as a "head rush." It is similar to the high from alcohol and other mind-altering drugs, and it is short-lived. Some people feel a brief sense of well-being. Some experience **hallucinations**. Slowed speech, a loss of muscle control, or giggling may also be part of the high.

When the high wears off, people feel drowsy and dizzy. They are often clumsy and unable to make good decisions. Some people pass out or have **seizures**. And sadly, an average of 125 people in the United States alone die each year from inhalant abuse. Accidents related to inhalant abuse cause almost half of these deaths. The rest are caused by **Sudden Sniffing Death syndrome**, or SSDS. In SSDS, the heart beats irregularly and then stops. Alarmingly, SSDS can happen even the first time someone uses inhalants. Twenty-two percent of those who die from SSDS are first-time users.

Inhalants cause permanent damage to the brain and body. The more inhalants a person uses, the worse the damage becomes. And inhalants are **addictive**. Many people suffer greatly from years of abuse.

Inhalants in the Body

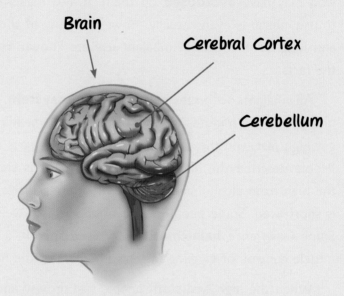

Brain

Cerebral Cortex

Cerebellum

Brain. Inhalants may dissolve the covering that protects your brain cells.

Cerebral Cortex. Inhalants kill cells in your cerebral cortex. This results in permanent personality changes, memory problems, and hallucinations. Damage here also causes learning disabilities.

Cerebellum. Inhalants damage your cerebellum. The damage affects your balance and coordination. It can slow down your speech and reduce muscle control. Long-term damage leads to tremors and shaking.

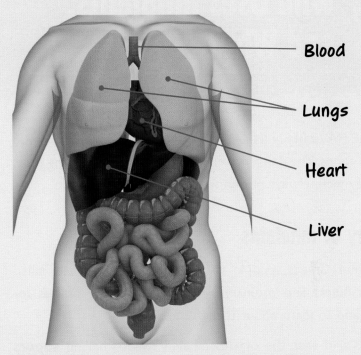

Blood

Lungs

Heart

Liver

Blood. Inhalants may limit the amount of oxygen that your blood can carry.

Lungs. When used repeatedly, inhalants damage your lungs and create breathing problems.

Heart. Inhalants can interrupt your heart's rhythm and cause immediate death.

Liver. Inhalants may cause liver damage, as a result of having to process toxic chemicals.

Other damage from inhalants includes:

Deafness. The cells that carry sound to the brain can die and leave you deaf.

Cancer. Some chemicals in inhalants have been shown to cause leukemia.

Weakness. Long-term inhalant use makes your muscles weaker and smaller.

Rashes. You may get "glue sniffer's rash," a bad rash around your nose and mouth.

2 Who Uses Inhalants, and Why?

PEOPLE HAVE BEEN INHALING FUMES TO GET HIGH SINCE ancient times. The dangers were misunderstood for a long time, but they were always present.

History of Inhalants

In ancient Greece, people visited **oracles** at a place called Delphi. Rulers and ordinary people went to the oracles for advice and to learn about their futures.

It is said that the oracles inhaled sweet-smelling **vapors** that drifted into their rooms. Then, they went into a **trance**. Sometimes, the vapors made the oracles act strangely, and some oracles died. Modern-day scientists believe the vapors were toxic gases from inside the earth, released by nearby earthquakes.

Most young people don't know about the dangers of abusing inhalants.

Thousands of years later, during the 1800s, people held parties to inhale the fumes of newly discovered gases. Doctors and scientists had just discovered nitrous oxide, ether, and chloroform. They were excited about the power these gases had, but they had not yet learned about the dangers. However, there were clues—some partygoers had bad reactions or became addicted.

Later, in the 1900s, many new products were invented as a result of the two world wars. And many of these products—such as motor oil, paint thinner, spray paint, and cleaning fluids—gave off fumes. Most people didn't breathe the fumes from these products on purpose. They were exposed to the fumes at work and became sick. People then realized that these fumes were toxic.

By the late 1900s, inhalant abuse had become a problem in the United States. In the 1960s, a glue-sniffing **epidemic** swept the country. In the 1970s, aerosol-sniffing became a big problem. The *New York Times* ran stories about the dangers of sniffing. Many other newspapers and many magazines did the same, and awareness about abuse grew. But today, inhalants are still often the first drugs that kids use.

sniffing: Breathing in an inhalant directly, through the nose.

bagging: Spraying or pouring the inhalant into a plastic bag and then breathing it in.

huffing: Spraying or pouring the inhalant into a cloth or rag and then breathing it in.

Dusting

Dusting is inhaling fumes from products people use to dust computer keyboards. Sometimes, people call this product "canned air." But don't be fooled by that name. This product isn't made of air. It's made of a mixture of chemicals that can be deadly when inhaled.

In December 2006, three teenage girls in Roseburg, Oregon, bought some duster spray. Then they got into a car, and took turns dusting. The car belonged to 16-year-old Ashley Jones. While she was driving, Ashley inhaled some duster spray, and then lost control of the car. The car flipped at least once before it slammed into a power pole. Both passengers were ejected from the car. Ashley was trapped inside.

Rescuers got Ashley out, but she died at the hospital. Her passengers both had severe injuries. One spent almost two months in the hospital.

Another "dusting while driving" accident happened in Little Rock, Arkansas. Shelby Armstrong smashed her car in a one-car accident. A can of computer duster was found at the scene. Less than a year later, Shelby drowned in her bathtub. The drowning was believed to be a result of dusting. It was January 2007. Like Ashley, Shelby was 16.

Who Abuses?

People from different places and different races seem equally likely to use inhalants. However, there are some things that many inhalant users have in common.

Young people who have lived below the **poverty line** are more likely to become long-term inhalant users than people who have not lived in poverty. People who have been sexually or physically abused, have poor grades, or have dropped out of school are also more likely to abuse inhalants regularly.

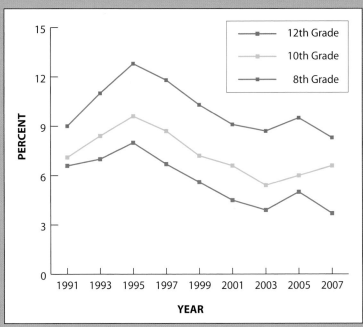

Percentage of U.S. Students Who Report Having Used Inhalants in the Past Year

Source: The Monitoring the Future Study, 2008

There are **gender** differences, too. In the fourth, fifth, and sixth grades, many more boys than girls experiment with inhalants. That changes in the seventh, eighth, and ninth grades, when boys and girls use inhalants equally. In high school and adulthood, inhalants are more popular with boys again.

The Question Is *Why?*

Inhalants cause real and lasting damage to minds, bodies, and lives, and yet millions of young people abuse them. Why?

Many inhalant users don't understand how dangerous inhalants are. They see inhalants at home, at school, and in stores, and they don't think of things that they see everyday as dangerous. But even people who have some idea of the risks don't always stay away from inhalants.

Some young people just enjoy the high. They love the rush and want to keep feeling it. Others are simply curious. They may hear people talk about bagging or sniffing and want to try it for themselves.

Peer pressure leads some to experiment with inhalants. Many kids try inhalants with their friends. They find it hard to say "no" when everyone around them is saying "yes." Opportunity is another big reason—inhalants are easy to find and cheap to buy. Users don't need to go through drug dealers to get inhalants. They don't have to hide them from adults, who are used to these everyday products being around.

But many people use inhalants for more emotional reasons. One reason people use inhalants is because they have hard lives. Getting high on inhalants helps numb their emotional pain. Using inhalants helps them forget about their problems, such as abuse, family struggles, hunger, or loneliness.

Of course, using inhalants doesn't fix any of these problems. And in fact, using inhalants can make things much worse. Sadly, by the time people realize that using inhalants is making them feel worse instead of better, they can't stop. They're addicted.

Researchers have recently discovered that inhalants are more addictive than they previously thought. This is because many inhalants work like other highly addictive drugs: cocaine and heroin. They go straight to the brain and create feelings of pleasure.

While they create this feeling of pleasure, however, they destroy nerves in the brain. This damage is permanent. And the more inhalants a person uses, the worse the damage is. This is a problem for many addicts and long-term users who need larger and larger amounts of inhalants to get the same high they used to get from smaller amounts.

Seth Bramley's mom used to find washcloths with her son's face outlined on them. They smelled like air freshener. She didn't know what the washcloths meant. Seth told her, "I don't want to get high, but I just can't stop." He realized he had a drug problem and he tried to get help, but his addiction was strong. Seth died after inhaling fumes from a can of shaving gel. He was 19 years old. "Seth was no longer in control," his mom said. "The inhalants had taken over his life."

Inhalant Abuse in Central America

In Central America, inhalant abuse is a huge problem. Tens of thousands of kids who live on the street sniff glue and other toxic products. Some of these kids are as young as five years old. Most of these kids live without parents. They dig around in dumpsters to find food to eat. They sleep in cardboard boxes. They beg on the street for change that they then use to buy glue. The glue they buy is made with toluene.

To Bruce Harris, the director of a shelter for kids in Central America, it makes sense that these kids would look for ways out of their pain. He says, "We see five-year-olds with their heads stuck in plastic bags because it takes away their hunger, it keeps them warm, and it replaces their teddy bear." Thirteen-year-old Luisa explained that sniffing glue helps her forget that she's hungry, homeless, and cold. She told a reporter, "When I feel nothing, I feel good."

Inhalant use in Central America is too often a downward spiral. Fourteen-year-old Amanda sniffed glue during her pregnancies. Her first daughter was born dead. Her second daughter had health problems. Amanda could not care for her daughter and abandoned her.

Joel lived on the streets in Guatemala. He started sniffing glue when he was eight years old. For years, he sang on buses for spare change. He used the change to buy food and glue. But by the end of his life, he bought only glue. He died before he was 17 years old.

Young children who are forced to live on the streets in Central America often turn to drugs to take away their hunger and help them forget their hard lives.

3 What's Being Done to Stop Inhalant Use?

AS MORE PEOPLE BECOME AWARE OF THE DANGERS OF inhalant abuse, more steps are taken to put an end to this problem. Today, there are laws in place about inhalant use. There are also treatment programs for those who need help breaking their addiction.

Laws and Inhalants

The laws about abusing inhalants vary from state to state. In some states, it is illegal to get high from inhalants. In other states, it is illegal to sell or give inhalants to people under 18 years old. Many states treat inhalants the same way they treat other drugs. A person is charged the same way for inhaling and driving as they would be for driving under the influence of alcohol or other drugs.

The laws about inhalant abuse vary from state to state.

State Laws About Inhalant Abuse

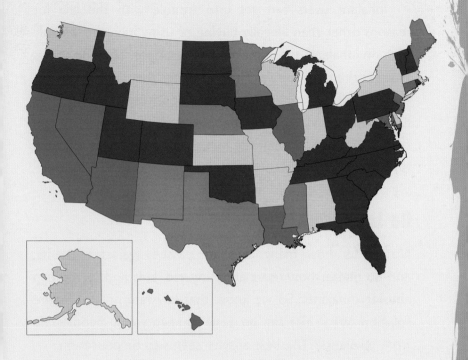

Here is how the different states handle inhalant abuse and sales:

Purple = In these states, it is illegal to use inhalants to get high.

Green = In these states, there are laws about selling inhalants to people under 18.

Pink = In these states, it is illegal to use inhalants to get high and/or there are laws about selling inhalants to people under 18. These states may also require businesses to post warnings about inhalants and write down the names of young people who buy them.

Gray = In these states, there are no laws about abusing or selling inhalants.

Source: The National Conference on State Legislatures, 2007, and the National Inhalant Prevention Coalition

Inhalant users can get into trouble with the law for reasons other than illegally buying or using inhalants. People high on inhalants often make poor decisions. They do things that get them in trouble. They do things that might even put them in jail. When a person is high on inhalants, bad ideas can sound good. Robbing people, stealing, or fighting can seem like fun. But when the high wears off, serving jail-time is no fun at all.

Do Laws Work?

No matter how many laws are passed against inhalants, and no matter how users are punished, kids and teens keep abusing inhalants. So we know that laws are not the entire solution. What else can be done to keep young people safe from inhalants? The best answer seems to be education.

If parents learn the signs of inhalant abuse, they can be more watchful. If kids realize the damage that inhalants can do to them, they can be smarter about resisting the urge to get high. If stores put up signs about inhalant abuse, everyone becomes more aware of the problem.

When people who have abused inhalants share their stories, they prove to everyone that inhalant abuse is a real problem and that it can happen to anyone. Education shows that the dangers are real, making people think twice before they experiment with inhalants.

Common Signs of Inhalant Abuse

- Problems at school, like falling grades and skipping classes

- An "I don't care" attitude

- No interest in friends, family, clothes, hobbies, or being clean

- Paint stains on body or clothes

- Spots or sores around the mouth

- Red, runny eyes or nose

- Breath that smells like chemicals

- Not very hungry

- Stomachaches

- Anxiety or excitability

- Being very easily annoyed

- Seeming drunk or dizzy

- Headaches

- Coughing

- Shaky hands

What About Treatment Programs?

Programs that treat inhalant addictions are fairly new. The first inhalant treatment center in the United States opened in Alaska in 2002.

Treatment for inhalant addicts is difficult. It takes a long time for most addicts to stop wanting to use inhalants. And many people who do stop eventually start using again. One reason for this is that inhalants are everywhere. After people leave treatment programs for other drugs, they try to avoid being around the drugs they were addicted to. It is nearly impossible for recovering inhalant addicts to avoid being around inhalants. But treatment programs can help.

Treatment programs for inhalant abuse have to treat both the body and the mind of the inhalant user. First, the body is treated. Patients take medical tests so that doctors can find out how much damage has been done to their bodies. These tests also tell doctors what chemicals are in the body. It takes two to six weeks just to get all of the chemicals out of a person's body.

Next, patients take tests to figure out how much damage has been done to their brains. Treatment sessions have to be short and simple. Patients don't have a normal attention span due to brain damage from inhalant use.

There are also sessions that address emotional issues, such as why the patient started using inhalants to begin with and how the patient will find support after treatment ends.

4 How to Help

YOU PROBABLY KNOW SOMEONE WHO IS ABUSING inhalants, whether or not you are aware of it. In the United States, one out of every five people has tried inhalants by the eighth grade. Chances are good that you actually know many kids who have tried inhalants. For this reason, it is a very good idea to learn the signs of inhalant abuse.

Once you are aware of someone's problem, you still might not want to talk to him or her about it. You might not want to tell an adult either. These are hard things to do. But it is much more difficult to watch someone you care about suffer damage or even die because he or she wouldn't accept or didn't know how dangerous inhalants are.

Talking about drug abuse is hard, but it can save a person's life.

Types of Users

If you or someone you know uses inhalants, figure out what kind of user you are or that person is. This knowledge can help you know what kind of help is needed. The four main types of inhalant users are:

- People between 10 and 16 who use inhalants with friends for a short period of time and then stop

- People between 10 and 16 who use inhalants alone for a short period of time and then stop

- People between 20 and 35 who have used inhalants with friends for five or more years

- People between 20 and 35 who have used inhalants alone for five or more years

The last two types of users typically have poor social skills and a limited education. They often have brain damage, as a result of using inhalants for a long time. Many have gotten into trouble with the law.

Treatment programs are aimed at long-term users, but remember, anyone who uses inhalants, even once, is in danger. No matter what type of user a person is, he or she needs help. If you are using inhalants or if someone you know is, talk to a parent, a teacher, or a counselor right away. Get information, and get help, to avoid an emergency.

In an Emergency

Sometimes inhalant use leads to an emergency. If you find a friend who is sick from inhalants or has overdosed:

1. **Don't panic.** Do not argue with or excite your friend. The stress could cause him or her to become more violent. It might even lead to SSDS.

2. **Call 911.**

3. **Open windows and doors.** Fresh air can help get rid of the fumes.

4. **Save anything you find that might tell doctors what your friend was inhaling.** This can be life-saving information.

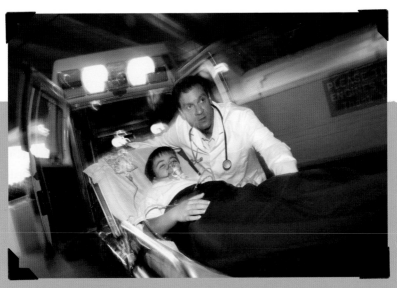

When inhalant users end up in the emergency room, they are generally very ill.

At the emergency room, medical staff will make sure the patient can breathe. They might give the person an oxygen mask or insert a tube into the lungs. They might do other tests, such as X rays, brain scans, and heart tests. These tests show how much damage the inhalant has already done to the patient.

If doctors know what the person inhaled, they can try certain treatments that work against the chemicals in that particular inhalant. If they don't know what was inhaled, there isn't much that doctors can do other than treat some of the symptoms, such as low blood pressure.

If the patient survives, he or she may spend up to five days getting over the overdose. During this time, the patient might experience **tremors**, nausea, pain, and hallucinations.

It Takes Courage

There are no easy ways to solve the problem of inhalant abuse. Many people think using inhalants feels good, so they keep using them. They tell themselves that nothing bad will happen. They tell themselves that the effects only last for a little while. But the fact is that inhalants can cause permanent damage or worse. And telling yourself, "That couldn't happen to me" does not change these facts.

If you have never tried inhalants, be glad. Tell other people about the dangers of sniffing, bagging, and huffing. If your friends pull out a can of duster spray or a bottle of glue, say "no thanks," and explain why.

If you are already using inhalants, talk to a grown-up about getting help. If you know someone else who is using, talk to that person about his or her inhalant use. These steps might be among the hardest things you will ever do. But they are acts of courage that can protect futures and save lives.

Robert's 13-year-old brother died of inhalant abuse. Only after his little brother's death did Robert learn what the warning signs were. "I wish that I could have told my brother [about inhalants]," he wrote. "Maybe if I had, he would have made a no-use decision… and he would be alive today."

GLOSSARY

addictive: Something that is difficult to stop using or doing.

central nervous system: The brain and spinal cord.

epidemic: Something that spreads widely and affects many people at one time.

gender: The sex (male or female) of a person or animal.

hallucinations: Sights, sounds, and other sensations that seem real but are not.

methylene chloride: A clear, colorless liquid that is used in paint thinners, spray cans, and other inhalants and is linked to many health problems.

oracles: People who are thought of as wise and able to see the future.

overdosed: Have taken too much of something, often a drug.

poverty line: The level of income (amount of money) it takes to pay for basic food, clothing, and shelter.

seizures: Sudden attacks of twitching muscles that are the result of a problem in brain activity.

Sudden Sniffing Death syndrome (SSDS): A possible effect of using inhalants, in which the heartbeat becomes irregular and then stops.

toluene: A clear, colorless liquid that comes from coal tar and crude oil and gives off fumes that can be toxic (poisonous).

toxic: Poisonous.

trance: The state of being so absorbed in an activity that nothing else is noticed.

tremors: Trembling or shaking typically caused by weakness or illness.

vapors: Fine substances that one can see floating in the air, such as a fog, mist, smoke, or gas.

FIND OUT MORE

Where to Get Help

National Inhalant Prevention Coalition
800-269-4237

Books

Flynn, Noa. *Inhalants and Solvents: Sniffing Disaster*. New York: Mason Crest, 2008.

Klosterman, Lorrie. *The Facts About Dependence to Treatment*. New York: Marshall Cavendish, 2008.

Marcovitz, Hal. *Drug Education Library–Inhalants*. New York: Lucent, 2005.

Menhard, Francha Roffè. *The Facts About Inhalants*. New York: Marshall Cavendish, 2005.

Robinson, Matthew. *Inhalant Abuse*. New York: Rosen Publishing Group, 2007.

Websites

Inhalant.Org
http://www.inhalant.org

National Inhalant Prevention Coalition
http://www.inhalants.org

National Institute on Drug Abuse for Teens: Inhalants
http://teens.drugabuse.gov/facts/facts_inhale1.php

Tips for Teens: Inhalants
http://ncadi.samhsa.gov/govpubs/phd631

INDEX

Page numbers for photographs and illustrations are in **boldface**.

abuse signs, 21, **27**
addictive (addiction), 7, 15, 22
aerosol, **4**, 5, 11
Alaska, 22
attention span, 22

blood, 9, **9**
brain, 8, **8**
    damage, 7–8, 15, 24
    cerebellum, 8, **8**
    cerebral cortex, 8, **8**

cancer (leukemia), 9
Central America, 16–**17**
central nervous system, 7
chloroform, 5, 11
correction fluid, 5
crime, 20

deafness, 9
death, 7, 9, 12, 15, 16, 25, 27
driving, 12, 18
dusting, 12

education, **10**, 14, 20, 24
emergency, 25–26
ether, 5, 11

gases, 5, 11
gender differences, 14
glue-sniffing, 11, 16

hallucinations, 7, 8, 26
heart, 9, **9**
heart failure (SSDS), 7, 25
help, 23–27, 30
history, 10–11

jail, 20

laughing gas. *See* nitrous oxide
laws, **18**, 18–20,
liver, 9, **9**
long-term use, 7, 8, 9
lungs, 6, 9, **9**, 26

methylene chloride, 6
muscles, 7, 8–9

nitrites, 5
nitrous oxide, 5, 11

overdose, 7, 25

paint thinners, 5
poverty, 13
pregnancy, 16

rash, 9

seizures, 7
solvents, volatile, **4**, 5, 6
spray paint, 5, 11
Sudden Sniffing Death
    syndrome (SSDS), 7, 25

toluene, 6, 16
treatment
    emergency, **25**, 25–26
    programs, 22, 24
tremors, 8, 26

users
    characteristics, 13–14
    in treatment, 22
    motivation, 14–17
    talking to, 23, **23**, 27
    types of, 24

whipped cream, 5
withdrawal, 26
world wars, 11